A

MASONIC ADDRESS,

DELIVERED

BEFORE THE WORSHIPFUL MASTER, OFFICERS AND BRETHREN,

OF THE

KENNEBECK LODGE,

IN THE

NEW MEETING HOUSE, HALLOWELL, MASSACHUSETTS;

JUNE 24th, ANNO LUCIS, 5797.

> The MASTER BUILDER, o'er the deep profound,
> Swift, on the wings of light'ning, roll'd the sound,
> "ANGLES! descend —dispel the shades of night"—
> Then gloomy CHAOS trembled into LIGHT!
>   Where the MASONIC PILLARS rise,
>   Contriv'd in WISDOM—and DESIGN—
>   Both STRENGTH and BEAUTY strike the eyes,
>   And ART and SYMMETRY divine!

BY BROTHER AMOS STODDARD.

HALLOWELL.
PRINTED BY BROTHER HOWARD S. ROBINSON.
A. D. *1797.*——— A. L. *5797.*

Festival of St. John, the Baptist, by the Kennebeck Lodge.

VOTED, That Brothers *George Warren, Ebenezer Brandish* and *Benjamin Whitwell*, be a committee to wait on Brother STODDARD, and to present him the thanks of the LODGE for the *elegant* and *masonic* Address, which he this day delivered, and to request a copy for the press.

Hallowell, June 24th, 5797.

Hallowell, 26th June 5797.

That my Address, on St. John's day, should meet the approbation of the KENNEBECK LODGE—before whom, and at whose request, it was delivered, excites my warmest gratitude. That it may possess *light*, and shine beyond the *East*, is the earnest wish of my heart—but the exercise of masonic candor and liberality will be necessary to cover its defects.

A. STODDARD.

A MASONIC ADDRESS.

Right Worshipful MASTER *and* BRETHREN !

ENGRAVEN on the masonic *Tablet* is this inscription, That the *inexperience* of a brother, claims a brother's indulgence; and that the errors of humanity, mixt with the best endeavors to serve the *craft*, are covered with the mantle of CHARITY.—Confiding in the truth of this remark, I appear before you in this place—to congratulate you on the return of this happy day, and the establishment of this *Eastern Heritage*—the *light* which directs the steps of the way-faring traveller—and to impart such hints as are compatible with the present solemnity.

Without discharging the demands of mutual dependence, mankind would live like brutes, and be the perpetual enemies of each other. The great difficulty is, to make them sensible of this dependence, and of their interest to obey its dictates. Our passions of sympathy and revenge often meet in collision—they constantly war in our breasts ; and while *truth* and *virtue* are contending for their proper empire, *vice* and *folly* alternately assume a frowning or ludicrous aspect, and either drive or laugh them into obscurity. Such are our passions by nature, and so much divided between duty and inclination, that our lives exhibit a strange mixture of good and evil : We heed not the dangers to which we are exposed, nor feel for the calamities of wretched man. To unfold and analyze these opposite propensities, is the great business of life : To bind the one in the cords of salutary restraint, and to expand the other on the wings of prudent discretion, are motives by which we ought to regulate our conduct. The attainment of happiness impels us to unite in the diffusion of KNOWLEDGE—in the inculcation of moral and divine precepts—in the practice of CHARITY—and in the acquisition of all the virtues which enoble and embellish human nature. Thus we learn to *square* our actions by the immutable dictates of reason, and to live within the *compass* of truth.

The multiplicity of our affections and the vast variety of our wants, will not suffer us to admit of gloomy solitude, nor of any exclusive prerogative over the bounties of providence. While the Arcadian state existed, so often the theme of poets, and the law of nature was the only rule of action, property had no permanent value : *Occupation* alone was the criterion of right. The subsequent establishment of civil society—the creation of fastidious distinctions, privileges, and exemptions, have cast the wealth of nations into the lap of indolence, and entailed a disgraceful servitude on the industrious community—plunged the more deserving into floods of misery and distress, and rendered them fit objects of BENEVOLENCE and CHARITY. Hence arises, in part, this moral obligation—*to feed the hungry, and to clothe the naked—to be of one mind— to have compassion one for another, and to love as brethren* of the same universal family.

But this observation would have little or no effect on the generality of men, were they not stimulated by the pride of example. There is a secret impulse in our nature, which constantly impels us to imitation; and virtuous and noble actions will ever be applauded, even by the profligate and abandoned. The charms of benevolence arrest the dissolute in the pursuit of pleasure, and he feels for the moment "*the milk of human kindness*" in his veins : he suddenly melts at the tale of woe—the tear of pity trembles in his eye—and then the deceptions and illusions of his past life sharpen the conviction of his mind.

To encourage these generous feelings—to give efficacy to resolutions of amendment, and to render them permanent in their operation, have ever been attended to by the patrons of masonic virture. They have given encouragement to learning and the arts among all the nations of the world—relieved the poor and distressed, and poured the balm of consolation into the wounds of suffering humanity. Such are the governing principles of the *ancient fraternity* of FREE and ACCEPTED MASONS ; and ADAM, our great progenitor, became the first GRAND MASTER on earth.

It is not my intention, neither would the limits of this discourse justify the attempt, to detail the historical rise and progress of masonry—but a glance at some of the most prominent features of the picture may be useful, and not unacceptable to those whom the novelty of our institution has drawn together on this occasion.

It is no presumption to say, that the masonic institution derives its origin from the Great MASTER BUILDER of the universe. The foundation of it was laid in the *eternal mind* anterior to the production of this material system, and the operation of it will extend into a boundless futurity.

DEITY conceived the vast design of creation—unbarred the gates of *light*—moulded all the terrene particles of matter into *form* and *figure*, and made MAN, the express image of himself— Lord paramount of all things here below. The SUN and MOON received a habitation in the heavens— the one to rule the day, and the other to rule the night. With wonderful *harmony* and *order* they began their revolutions—each performed an exactitude of part—both operated to the same end; and unbounded creation united in aspirations of homage to the SUPREME ARCHITECT of heaven and of earth.

Placed in the bowers of paradise, our first parents felt no apprehension of evil—no solicitude at their future fate—no fling of remorse to wound their peace. The contemplation of the works of nature was a source of delight; and their elevated conceptions of the divine *wisdom* and *goodness*—their intimacy with heaven, and its celestial inhabitants, rendered them unsuspicious of lurking danger. One solitary act of disobedience crowned their misery—doomed them to a vast variety of untried scenes, and entailed a complicated mass of *evil* on their posterity. Wrapt in the dunest curtains of solitude, they had only a partial discovery of that *light* which before beamed around them with lustre. They beheld the majesty of an angry GOD—found themselves secluded from his presence—condemned to seek protection in *manual labor*, and to gain subsistence by the *sweat of the brow*. Creation exhibited a dreary and unfruitful waste : The midnight howlings of beasts of prey, and the convulsions of nature, filled their mind with terror—the scorching sun-beam, and the wintry blast, dictated the necessity of convenient shelter. The works of nature, though disfigured by noxious weeds, and by frightful eruptions, unfolded the elements of GEOMETRY ; and their immediate wants suggested the means of present security. The seeming desertion of omnipotence, and the black catalogue of *evils* to which they were exposed, induced the early male inhabitants of the globe to *operate with design*, and to aim at improvement in the requisite sciences. To effectuate this purpose, they eventually founded a LODGE on *the East of Eden*, which our adorable GRAND MASTER delighted to honor. The rays of *light*, remaining at the dawn of man's depravity, were sufficient to point out an indissoluble connection between virtue and happiness—vice and misery ; and the "ROYAL ART," the emanation of DEITY himself, and registered in heaven's chancery, was ordained to discriminate between them—to draw us to the one, and induce us to flee the other.—Here then unfolds the great duty of masons—to aid and love one another—to run our course in FAITH—to lean on the pillars of HOPE—and to be constant in the diffusion of CHARITY—to practice all the sublime, moral and social virtues, and to set a bright example to the rest of mankind. Hence it follows, that the LODGE here below is a *type* and *shadow* of the GRAND LODGE above ; and that the nearer we approach *perfection*, the more we resemble that *adorable original*.

The first rudiments of our institutions were inculcated in the LODGE on *the East of Eden*, and all mankind united in their pursuit of KNOWLEDGE. Their objects were—to discover the extent and precision of all the useful and ornamental arts, and to impress on the mind the importance of moral and religious duties ; the one was necessary to the convenience and protection of this life— the other to a well grounded prospect of a pleasurable *refreshment* within the *vail*. By an assiduous attention to these primary objets of the institution, one found out the method of working in stone and lime—another invented musical instruments, and a third became acquainted with the use of metals, and constructed implements of husbandry. The LODGE dwelt together in unity of spirit—and the bonds of peace were held essential to the progressive improvement of the *craft*.

But how weak and unsubstantial are the most sacred ties! How fleeting the joys of social man! The voice of *murder* interrupted the LODGE! A detestable *fratricide* existed! A brother's blood soaked from the ground, and ABEL fell the victim!

The commission of this premeditated crime, compelled CAIN, and his coajutors in iniquity, to retire into *the vallies below*—induced them to build a strong city *in the land of strangers*, where *they had fellowship with the unfruitful works of darkness*. The *true* and *faithful* still dwelt in *the holy mountain* : They expelled the impious and immoral, and adopted a scrupulous precaution in the admission of future members. From this period a discrimination took place ; and the *light* has only reached the *patient* and *benest labourer*, to whom is committed " *the secret of finding out arts.*"— The knowledge of the institution, previously acquired by the fratricide and his family, was soon buried in oblivion ; and their exclusion from the *secret rites* of the fraternity, rendered the transmission of it impracticable.

Complicated are the designs of DEITY, and wonderful are the operations of his hand. Instead of *light*, he sometimes buries the world in darkness—Instead of peace and prosperity, he sends war and pestilence among the nations, and permits the propagation of the vilest depravity, as a substitute for more important good. The heart demoralized, and the hasty progress of vice, the sure harbinger of some fatal calamity, at length caused an union of the inhabitants of the *vale* and *mountain*, and the precious traits of moral rectitude were absorbed in an ocean of corruption—a period was put to virtuous and useful improvement, and the wrath of heaven was ready to burst on a devoted world. Only one family among the sons of men retained the favor of Omnipotence, and found protection in the moment of calamity. When the heavens gathered blackness, and a flood of waters prevailed on the earth—when all nature trembled to its centre, and the nations were sinking in the tomb of destruction, this HOUEHOLD OF FAITH sate secure in their LODGE—smiled at the mighty billows, and saw the bursting storms discharge their contents without apprehension of danger.

The frowning tempest lulled, and "the waters of oblivion" dried up, "the wreck of matter, and the crust of worlds," exhibited a melancholy aspect ; and the spectacle of a shattered globe, then a wild and gloomy desert, extorted the look of terror, mixt with pity and compassion. The proudest temples and pyramids were in one mingled ruin—and all the monuments of *art* and *skill* were lost in the general confusion, save one lonely pillar of ENOCH in the land of *Siriad*—on which was inscribed the *mysteries of the craft*—a faithful transcript of the *tressel-board* of Eden—and its characters remained legible so late as the second century.* This marble column, the handy-craft of masterly genius, long braved

---

*Josephus Ant. quoted in Univ. Hist. 1, 169

the injuries of time—stood as a pillar of *light in the East*, and pointed out the footsteps of ancient masonic wisdom.

The family of NOAH soon multiplied into a great nation, and the whole circle of the useful and ornamental arts was revived among them : The *wife* and *expert* were early formed into LODGES —the *mysteries* explained, and *secrecy* enjoined. They have left us indubitable evidence of their *skill* in works of *magnificence* and *taste*, and their immediate successors of moral improvement. Witness the splendid structure of *Belus*, and the numerous cities *in the East*, founded by *Nimrod* and *Nimus* *—the pyramids, temples, and columns in *Egypt*, attributed to *Sesostris*, and to subsequent princes— the almost infinite variety of porticoes, amphitheatres, and other public edifices, in ancient Greece and Rome : —Witness the curious remains of *Telecles* and *Theodorus*,† the most famous statuaries of antiquity ;—still they draw us to the sculptured monument, or to the ruins of some ancient city—point us to the mouldring productions of genius, and bid us imitate their *wisdom, strength* and *beauty*—not only for temporary convenience, but for the more lasting improvement and embellishment of the mind :—Witness the detached and mutilated precepts of *Pythagoras* and *Plato* ;— they still point us out the origin and essence of masonry—unfold the secret springs of human action, and of moral rectitude, and

*Univ. Hist. 1, 279 & 4, 279
† Ibid   1. 504

all the hidden treasures of nature ; still they inculcate the duties of moral life, and open the gates of scientific KNOWLEDGE. *Euclid* daily affords new lessons of instruction, and the scholar derives *pleasure* and *profit* in the solution of his problems. Still *Archimedes* is engaged in the defense of his country—we trace him on the walls of *Syracuse*—we see him repel, by his superior *skill* in the *arts*, the efforts of a veteran army—draw down the lightning of heaven, and consume the proud navies of Rome : *—Witness also the Patriarchs and Apostles of old ; they still exhibit the *sign* of MASTER MASONS, and *bear faithful witness of the light* : We inculcate their precepts, and recommend their examples—and happy ! thrice happy he, who regulates his conduct by them.

Worthy here is the remark, that the confusion of tongues and the dispersion of families at the building of *Babel*, very much reduced the primitive KNOWLEDGE of the *craft*—for the milder arts of peace, and useful learning, gave way to the savage manners of men, and to the infuriate ravages of war.†

But the most necessary discoveries were never entirely lost : The precious art of *designing* and of *building* was preserved by the families that remained in *the land of Shinar* ; and by them eventually transmitted to the several branches of the dispersion. It was revived in all its lustre under the most celebrated *artist* in Israel ;

*Univ. Hist. 8, 147 † Goguet's origin, Ac. 1. 3.

and the temple of *light*, erected on Mount Moriah, where the great MASTER BUILDER established his *glory in the midst of his people*, is ample proof of this declaration.

Pertinent too is the remark, that MASONRY seeks the lonely shade, designed for contemplation, and declines at the approach of war, and mental darkness. At one period in Great Britain, it was considered by the vulgar and illiterate as a species of sorcery, and its votaries were loaded with epithets of approbium and disgrace; at a second, it was attacked by the formality of an act of Parliament;*—and at a third, it was menaced by the malediction of an imperious and jealous Queen†. The time at length arrived, when kings and princes, as well as the dignitaries of the church, conceived it an honor to have their names enrolled on the masonic catalogue.

The *mysteries* of the *craft* were introduced into Europe by the progeny of GOMER, the eldest son of *Japhet* , who pealed *all the western Isles.*‡ In these early times, the *Druids* held the keys of KNOWLEDGE : Their office among the northern nations was sim-

---

* During the minority of Henry the fifth in 1425, an act passed, declaring it felony for the Masons to confederate in Chapters or Congregations. But this act, obtained by the craft of a disappointed Priest, was never put in force, and was very soon virtually repealed by subsequent statutes.

† Queen Elizabeth, understanding that the Masons were possessed of secrets, which they would not impart, sent a troop of horse to disperse the LODGE at York in 1561—but being informed that to support the existing government was a tenet of the order, she desisted from the enterprise by recalling these ministers of her vengeance.

‡ Univ. Hist. 1, 375 & 6, 6

ilar to that of the *Magians* of *Egypt*, who preserved their *mysteries* by *figures* and allegorical *emblems*, sculptured in wood, or engraven on metallic substances. In imitation of the Patriarchs of old, they held their LODGES under the branches of some AGED OAK ; and to avoid an exposition of their *secret rites*, and to prevent the infliction of criminal justice, the consequence of discovery, they assembled on the *highest hills*, or in the *lowest vallies*.

The world has ever been in pain to explore the *secrets* of the *craft*. Invention and subtilty, menaces and tortur, have been alternately employed, by fanaticism and ignorance, to gain an exposition—but all in vain : Like a mighty rock in the ocean, the masonic institution stands unhurt amid the storms of passionate imposition —it bids defiance to the angry surge which dashes against its tide, and dies at its feet ! Jealousy and envy, two powerful engines, have even conjured up a multiplicity of demons, and placed them in the temple of concord, the sacred retreat of *friendship* and *virtue*, as the guardians of our nocturnal deliberations. Religion too has put in her claim, and arrogates to herself the right of excommunication. Our *secret rites* have provoked the ingenuity of punsters—the whole artillery of libels—and the grave and solemn admonitions of the pulpit.* Happy for us, were we able to impress on the public mind this serious Truth, That the ma-

---

*The more enlightened Clergy of the present day are too liberal in their sentiments to be criminated by this observation. I here allude to the Clergy of past times when they exercised despotic domination over temporal princes, and priest-craft controlled the affairs of state.

sonic institution is founded in FAITH, HOPE, and CHARITY—and that *the love of all mankind* forms one of the most essential pillars of it—then the propriety of that seal on our lips, which secures the treasures of our KNOWLEDGE, would be viewed with indulgence, and the importance of *secrecy* more easily evinced. The professors of every science have their *secrets*.—The great and complicated affairs of nations, and the minuter transactions among men, require *secrecy* ; and the *Arcana* of heaven is impenetrable to man. Among the Romans it was death to divulge the *secrets* of state : Neither the hope of reward, nor the apprehension of tortur, could *unseal* the sacred deposit ; and instances occur in history, where victims, faithful to their truth, have either bit off their tongues to avoid utterance, or expired in silent agony under the scorge of despotism. This affords an important lesson to modern politicians—some of whom have violated this ancient *Rescript*—have imposed a serious aspect on important trains of negociation by *imprudent* and *untimely* discoveries.

How far this mode of reasoning will apply to the *secrets* of masonry, masons alone can determine. It will at least prove this fact to all, that *secrecy* is many times necessary ; and as no evils have ever resulted from this sublime institution, but on the contrary much apparent good, the *private tenets* of the fraternity ought to have a favorable construction.

Ye curious and inquisitive, without the pale of the fraternity, beware of the judgement ye pass on the utility of Masonry merely by the *fruits* of some unworthy professors. If this be the criterion of praise or censure, what will become of the christian system ? A similar objection might be made, with equal propriety, to all the great doctrines of the BIBLE : Most men acknowledge them—and yet how few obey their divine precepts !

But if we look into the history of mankind, and trace out the fruits of masonry in all their connections and dependencies, we shall be convinced that no description of men in society has ever been more deserving. Their principles are calculated to stop the progress of vice—to unfold and enforce the great duties of religion and morality. The institution is properly divided into two parts—*operative* and *speculative*. *Operative* masonry alludes to the useful rules of architecture—whence a structure derives *figure*, *strength* and *beauty*, and a just proportion in all its parts : —It also displays the influence, and evinces the fund of human *wisdom* and *ingenuity*, implanted in man, equal to all the salutary purposes of life. *Speculative* masonry is of a more sublime nature—and points out our duty to ourselves, to our neighbor, and to our GOD : It leads us to contemplate with admiration the works of nature, and fills the mind with the most elevated conceptions of the divine purity.*

---

* Vide Perison's Illustrations—page 10—from whence part of the preceding paragraph is extracted.

In conformity to these principles, the *true* Mason pursues the dictates of justice, temperance, fortitude, charity and brotherly kindness : He is as wise as the serpent, and as harmless as the dove. These enable him to set an example of good to the community—to preserve the vigor of his mental powers, so as to investigate the EUREKA*—to persevere in the performance of duty, and to be encouraged as difficulties encrease—to enter the cottage of poverty and distress—to dispense his bounty to the poor, and to dry up the tears of affliction : He acknowledges one supreme Governor of the world, and never mentions his name but with reverence and respect : He *squares* his conduct by the precepts of the divine and moral law, and always keeps a tongue of *good report*. These principles were established at the first dawn of *light in the East*, and govern, at this day, every legitimate LODGE under Heaven. Christians, Jews, Turks, and even the untutored Savages, feel and acknowledge their influence. They can all assemble at the alter, and mutually salute by the tender name of *brother*. Unacquainted, perhaps with each others vernacular dialect, they can keep up a reciprocal intercourse, and interchange of sentiment, by a *distinct, artificial* and *figurative* language, peculiar to themselves, and understood by the fraternity in all parts of the globe. The The expressive language of the LODGE on *the East of Eden*, conveyed to the NOACHIDE *in the land of Shinar*, and from them

---

* "The 47th of the first book of Euclid; which, if rightly understood, is not only the found-
" ation of masonry, but of all proportions and dimensions whatsoever."

transmitted to the MASTER BUILDERS on Mount Moriah, has been handed down, thro' successive ages, without even the shadow of a change.

The *fruits* of masonry appear with equal lustre in the works of *genius* and of *skill*. Notwithstanding the dismemberment of Empires, and the lapse and revolutions of time, the remains of antiquity still point out the footsteps of masonic *wisdom*. Who can reflect on the shattered piles of monumental labor in *the Eastern States*, without droping the tear of pity at the degeneracy of mankind ? Who can behold the moss-grown pyramids of Egypt, whose tops were almost buried in the clouds—who can traverse the disorganized ruins of temples, porticoes and columns, which were once great, but are now no more, without cursing the ruthless hand of tyranny, and the ravages of barbarism ? Who can realize the utter extinction of that magnificent structure of *light* on the Mount at Jerusalem, and feel not the force of its MASTER BUILDER'S inscription—*all is vanity beneath the Sun* ?

As the masonic institution flourishes most in the perfection of the arts—of course the jaring discord of contending nations is the bane of its growth, and inflicts a temporary wound. O that the dove, with an olive branch in her beak, might be seen to fly again in our borders—and the blasting mildew of untoward incidents, and the tempest of national disaffection, mitigate their rage.

Europe still swims in blood, and the raven croaks hoarse in foreign climes. The proudest prince trembles on his throne, and the Roman Pontiff, the scourge of christendom, with speed precipitates the Vatican. O that the temple of *Janus** might be once more shut, and its gates be fastened by adamantine bars! But vain the wish! The brazen throat of war must be glutted with blood of nations, and then peace will establish her empire on earth. The Lord of Hosts rides in the whirlwind, and directs the storm!

Our illustrious GRAND MASTER, directed by the *Compass* of duty, hath exchanged the toils of state, for the more pleasing scenes of domestic life. Chearfully would I bestow an elogium on that exalted character : others might receive it on a just comparison with some celebrated chief of antiquity—but how can the SUN derive additional lustre from the beams of a STAR!

A few words to you, Right Worshipful MASTER *and* BRETHREN, *and I shall close this address.*

THE fiery steeds of time rush swiftly on. The period is at hand *when the wolf shall dwell with the lamb, and the leopard lie down with the kill—when the people that walk in darkness shall see a great* LIGHT, and universal KNOWLEDGE commence her reign.

---

* Numa Pompilius, Emperor of Rome, built a temple, and dedicated it to Janus.—It looked two ways, and examined past and future events—it was designed as a symbol of prudence—and stood open in times of war, and was shut in times of peace. Between the period of its foundation and the christian era, it was shut up five times: —the first time, in the days of Numa—the second, at the end of of the Punic war—the third, under Caesar Augustus, after the defeat of Marc Antony, and the death of Cleopatra—the fourth, on the reduction of the Coniberians or Cantabrians, in Spain—and the fifth, at the time of our Saviour's birth, when "There was peace over all the land." The temple was afterwards twice shut in the reigns of Nero and Vespasian—and opened, probably for the last time, by the Emperor Gordian.

We are placed in the world as children of the LIGHT ; and therefore let our GOOD WORKS so shine before men, that others may be induced to follow our example. We are not only members of our *mystical* body, but GOLDEN CANDLESTICKS in the masonic *Zion*.

Convince the world by our conduct, that the masonic institution leads to *virtue*, and to the acquisition of every *noble* accomplishment. To preserve it pure and unblemished, suffer no man of *evil report* to pass thro' the gates into the city. Impress this truth on the minds of all, That the ascent to our Temple of concord is steep and difficult ; and that the way-faring traveller must *ask* before he can receive—must *seek* before he can find—and must *knock* before the doors can be opened for his reception.

Support the government under which we live, and be obedient to the laws.

Pay due defference to the *requisitions* and *instructions* of the MASTER, and other Officers—and study to preserve the ancient *land-marks* of our order.

Ridicule not the curiosity of the most amiable part of creation. Give them to understand, that they were not designed to preside in the council of state nor to command in fields of blood ; and that a *free and accepted* MASON is under a double obligation to *love* and *protect* them.

Our progress in masonic virtue is attended with difficulties. Our baser passions, like the ocean in a storm, exceed the bounds prescribed them by right reason, and interrupt our laudable pursuits : but with a firm and magnanimous resolution, let us cling to the PILLARS of our *trust* :—Let us enter Aprentices to FAITH—Fellow-crafts to HOPE—and, as masters, forget not CHARITY ; and then if, like the faithful Son of the poor Widow of old, we perish in the day of calamity, by the hands of brutal ruffians, our end will be glorious and happy.

Remember the poor and needy : *cast your bread on the waters*—for verily I say unto you, reward cometh in the end. In all things, let us act up to the principles of our profession—for in so doing we are sure to find a *home* in every country, and a *friend* in every brother.

Be careful to imitate the serpent in his *wisdom*—the dove in her innocence —the ants and bees, in their industry.

While therefore, we walk as children of the DAY, let us bear in mind the *night* of death, which will put a period to all our pursuits ; and be prepared to enter the GRAND TEMPLE OF LIGHT above—not made with hands—eternal in the heavens !

Reprinted by Robert Stoddard Publishing
2019
Every effort has been made to duplicate the original work and to respect authenticity.
Grammar, spelling, punctuation and formatting are as original.
Any errors in this reprint are intentional.

To Order Additional Copies, Contact:
Robert Stoddard Publishing
rob.stoddard@hotmail.com

www.ingramcontent.com/pod-product-compliance
Lightning Source LLC
Chambersburg PA
CBHW071419290426
44108CB00014B/1890